I ... be kind!

With thanks to
Catherine Veitch and Jean Claude.

Miles Kelly

Far away, in a land of ice and snow, lived a colony of emperor penguins.

The penguin chicks were growing fast and needed lots of food.

Pippi's chick was called Ella and
she always had the most food.

Pippi knew where to
find the tastiest food,
but kept it a secret.

One day, Pippi let her friend Pita follow her to a high, icy cliff.

Pippi did a spectacular dive into the water.

Pita was very scared, but he had a chick to feed too.

Pita threw himself into the water and Pippi laughed when he splash-landed.

All penguins are better at swimming than walking.

But Pippi was a particularly good swimmer.

Huff, puff!

Pita struggled to keep up with her!

Pippi led Pita to where there was plenty of krill, which is a penguin's favourite food.

They ate and ate.

When it was time to go, Pippi raced to a hole in the ice and leapt out. Pita was much slower...

...and Pippi spotted an orca nearby.

Pippi dived back into the water to lead the orca away from Pita.

She swum the fastest she had ever swum in her life.

It was a long while before it
was safe for Pippi to come back.

Pita's chick was enjoying a
delicious meal of mashed-up
krill when Pippi arrived.

Now Pippi could feed Ella too.

But where was Ella?

Ella was nowhere to be seen.

All the penguins helped Pippi look for Ella.

What a relief when they found her buried under a big pile of snow!

"A huge bird swooped down and scared me," said Ella. "So I hid."

Pippi was so grateful to the other penguins for helping to find Ella.

The next day, Pippi kindly showed everyone where to find food.

She taught them to slide, dive, swim and leap, just like her.

Soon the penguin chicks would be big enough to go off on their own.

But for now, it was important the penguins be kind and look after each other.

Can you think of a time when you were kind and helped someone?